The Little Touch

© Natalie Kimbrough, Healing ISIS, 2010

This is dedicated to life – the beautiful experience here on earth that sometimes appears like a rollercoaster but always provides us with new hope…somehow.

This is also dedicated to all those who resonate with any of the emotions expressed – you are not alone!

I am grateful for the gift of expression and sharing and all the inspirational lessons I have and continue to learn.

Thank you to the one who's supporting me and showing me so much love and accepts me the way I am – every day, I am truly blessed. "Ever since"
…

Peace & Love,
Natalie

I: Shadow & Light

The Little Touch	7
Your Green Eyes	8
Awaken	9
Changes	10
Thinking	11
Wanting	12
Life's Storage Box	13
Me?	14
Manual Transmission	15
Little Things	17
Outside	18
The Strange Dance	19
The Sun	20
Thinking	21
This fear	23
This feeling	24
Where are the colors?	25
Soul mate? (1)	26

II: Misery & Ecstasy

You are	29
When I leave	31
Polar Opposites	32
All the Reasons	33
Come Tomorrow	35
The First Time	36
With Me	37
Heaven	39
Can't help myself	40
Conditioning	42
Lonely Too Long	44
Emotions Amok	46
Ever Since	47
The Road	49
How not to end?	50
Forbidden Fruit	52
Hard to Bear	53
Miracle	54
When you look at me	55
Never Before	57

One Dance	58
Physically and emotionally	60
Spring and Summer – Breaking Point	61
Surprise Attack	63
Timing	64
Trembling	65
Until Then	66
Will you?	68
Breaking	70
Writing	71
'Til Death…	73

I: Shadow and Light

The little touch

Your soft touch
When you come
To lie on my arm
Tells me that you care

Your little push
When my arm is
Not in the right position
Tells me you love me

Your soft sigh
When you close your eyes
While lying on my arm
Tells me that you trust me

Your soft voice
When I enter the room
And you see me
Tells me you've been waiting

Your loving look
When you see I am
Not feeling so good
Tells me that you understand

Your slow touch
Of your soft paw
Onto my head
Tells me that you are there

Your quick jump
Onto my lap
When I need someone to hold
Tells me that you will never leave.

Your Green Eyes

Your green eyes
Are looking at me
Insistently
Questioning...

Your green eyes
Are looking at me
Seeing
My soul

Your green eyes
Are looking at me
With so much love
And dedication

Your green eyes
Are telling me
That you understand
All of me

Your green eyes
Are telling me
That you see me
For who I am

Your green eyes
Are warm and loving
And always knowing
What I am feeling

Your green eyes
Are all I need
To find my balance
And feel loved.

Awaken

Do you see the tree
Oh – can it be?
Have you ever seen
Such deep, shining green?
Just open your mind

I wonder why
Suddenly the sky
Seems so much lighter
And life so much brighter
Than you normally find.

And there's some yellow
The mood's no longer mellow
The mind starts to dance
Thoughts cross that fence
Which sleepiness has built.

Oh – look around
Have you never found
Such colorful day
Shone by the sun's single ray
My heart's now filled with joy.

Suddenly we realize
That opening our eyes
We are waking up
We can no longer stop
Because spring awakens all.

Changes

A different city
A different country
A different life
Are those really changes?

A different voice
A different language
A different job
Are those really changes?

A different car
A different house
A different last name
Are those really changes?

A different me –
that has not yet happened
so what is the talk about
when you say there are so many changes in me?

Thinking

I was just thinking –
    About yet another name,
    Another name for a cat –
    No. 5
I was just thinking –
    About yet another dinner,
    Another dinner for us –
    Why bother?
I was just thinking
    About yet another load of laundry,
    Another laundry day
    Another Sunday.
I was just thinking –
    About yet another grocery list
    Another run to the grocery store,
    The fridge is half empty.
I was just thinking –
    About yet another thought,
    So I won't feel again
    What else is there?
Thinking – another painkiller: reason.

Wanting...

What is it you want?
It's hard to tell
Since you don't like sharing
your thoughts and feelings with me.

What do you need?
I would hope it is me
But if often seems that I
am standing in your way.

What do you wish?
Oh – do you even know
Because you sure can't show
And here I am outside the playing field.

But you know,
What I want is you
- you completely --
Not just a piece here and there.

Wanting you –
Is hard to do
Because you don't want to give;
What I want most.

Life's storage box

The rain is falling
All are waiting for
The first snow.

I laugh
I feel fine
I would like to please others
I could embrace the whole world
I could sing out loud
I could dance in the street
- then I see you.

Suddenly all has changed.
My hands begin to freeze
My voice is gone
My knees threaten to give way.
I love you,
But you don't know.

What else does life has in store?

Me?

Friendly,
Kind,
Helpful,
Fun.

Reliable,
Punctual,
Sociable,
Honest.

Responsive
Responsible,
Respectful,
Giving.

Dependable,
Trustworthy,
Sociable,
Earnest ...

How come I don't see myself like that?

Manual Transmission

Left hand on the steering wheel
The head is suddenly make that movement to
the left
The fingers of the hand start moving – slightly
Then they grab the steering wheel tighter.

Right hand on the transmission
Suddenly grabbing it real tight,
While the fingers of the left are moving
The grab tightens

Left hand taking hold of the steering wheel
Left foot hitting the pedal hard,
Right hand -- suddenly
Shifting into the next gear – violently

Left hand holding on tightly – with ease
Right hand hovers over the shifting stick
Right foot hitting the gas – all the way
Only to be taken off

For the left food hitting the pedal
To shift into yet a higher gear
With the small engine
Screaming in delight at the speed

Both eyes focused on the road ahead
With the car speeding forward,
Left and right foot in easy harmony
With the demands of manual transmission

Suddenly the fingers of the left hand ...
Start moving again ....
The right hand lifts - relaxing
The eyes look at the speedometer...

The ease and power of driving,
Having gotten lost in my mind
Driving this hard - automatically
What did I try to do?

Little things

Little things
To which I have
Gotten used to
This past year –
Taken for
Granted
Begin to
Sadden me
Because
I now experience them
More intensely,
Because I sense
That these
Little things
Are what I will
Miss enormously -
At home.

It seems
As if
Little things
Can often have
A great impact.

Outside

I am
Amidst a group of people
We all share
Some common interests
Yet,
It seems:
I don't belong.

I am
Amidst a group of friends
We all share
So many things
Yet,
It seems:
I don't belong.

I am
Amidst my family
We all care and share
Our lives, hopes and dreams
Yet,
It seems:
I don't belong.

It seems
That wherever I am
I am always,
On the outside –
Looking in.

The Strange Dance

See them dance
Taking their chance
Jumping around,
Wildly on the ground --
The harmony is striking.

Hear the music now
My head I ant to bow
To the natural rhyme
In this dance of time --
This is much to my liking.

Close your eye
Before the goodbye
Of this grand show --
soon the dancers will flow
Down the street.

Where man without a thought
Will not be distraught
Because they gave it a name
And want to get out of the rain
Trampling beauty with their feet.

The sun

The sun
Shine in my face
With such enormous grace
I can only stand in awe
Just like every time before

The sun
Shows what is around me
In a place I don't want to be
But this were you are, too
Oh – this cannot be true.

The sun
Wants to brighten my day
Instead I can only pray
That this day will soon end
Because I am already so bent

And the sun
Does not give up
To shine inside my room
But I only feel enormous doom –
Is there hope in the sunlight?

Thinking….

The wedding was sweet
I could feel my heart beat
The love was everywhere
a very special kind of air.

Yet, I was there alone
Has my despair shown?
I wished for you to be there
But I couldn't find you anywhere.

My emotions began to run wild
But my appearance was mild
I hated you so much
and missed, terribly, your touch.

I wished for us to be near
But there always is this fear
That you don't want me that way
And I wouldn't know what to say.

I've always been fine – alone
But now I'm always prone
To missing you
- there's nothing I can do.

I wished you could have listened
As her father's words glistened
Maybe you would find out
That's what it's all about.

But you don't seem
To share this dream
So I keep my hopes inside
      - wishing you'd see the light.

That I come to be
What you are to me
The sun in my life
And for commitment
We will strive.

This fear….

For a few days
I have been feeling
a great fear inside of me.

The fear
That my friends have changed,
That we won't know what to say,
That we will have distanced ourselves,
Without knowing,
Without wanting…

The fear
That I will not be able to get used to
My hometown – anymore.

The fear
That I will have to bury
All my dreams.

But the greatest fear
That I won't get along anymore
With my family
Because in the end
It is me
Who has changed.

This feeling

I am afraid
Of my feelings,
Which sometimes
Amaze me in their depth.

I am afraid
Of my ambition,
Which sometimes
makes it hard
To relax.

I am afraid
Of my pride,
Because it often hinder me
to give in to my feelings.

I am afraid
Of my insecurity,
Because it does not fit the picture,
which I paint for others.

I am afraid
Of getting hurt
So I often act
So strange
       - maybe even arrogant.

Dear God, I am afraid of myself!

Where are the colors?

Are my eyes open?
It's all so dark and rainy,
It's all so cloudy and grim,
Where have I been?

My eyes are open wide,
Yet – there are no colors around
It's grey, in grey, in grey…
What a saddening day.

My eyes turn to the right,
Still a colorless world
Then I see your face
But I am still caught in a daze;

My eyes are open,
My heart is not
It has been torn
completely worn

There used to be colors
In this world for me
But not now
Because I cannot start
To see the colors
When my body and mind
Are drained,
From all the demands
The world makes
So you will just keep me
in this dark, colorless place.

Soul mate? (1)

Coming home
You look at me
With your deep green eyes
Looking into my soul
To determine
How I feel.

Coming to the table
You tilt your little head
And stretch your head towards me
Figuring out my emotions
To determine
What to do.

Touching our soft hair
You stretch your neck further
And react to my touch
Your move is intentional
To determine
What I need

Looking into your eyes
And greeting you with my voice
You know exactly
What I need
And will – without questions
Give what I need.

Walking away to change
I know fully well
That without anything discussed
Whether I am aware of it or not
You will provide me
With what I need today –
Again.

Coming home and looking at you
I can't help but wonder:
Is it possible
For a cat
To be my soul mate?

II: Misery and Ecstasy

You are ...

Was it an accident that we met?
On that I would not bet;
It seems more like fate to me.

We seem to have come close
And that is why I pose
This for you to see:

Why do you need to apologize
For things that in your eyes
Are at the moment right?

You should not have to explain
When you want to go insane --
It should not be a fight.

Sometimes you wonder why
You just want to cry
But it is only fair;

You've had it rather rough --
Had to become pretty tough
And your heart needs care.

You have a achieved a lot
And you have another shot
at life in bliss.

What seems to clear to me,
You don't want to see --
I wonder why that is...

You have so much to give
But sometime you forget to live
And just wonder how.

Embrace your pain
And take love's lane
to yourself right now.

Your family will understand
And scars you will mend
If you are yourself --
Because only then you are - perfect.

When I leave….

To my surprise
Tears fill my eyes
When I look at you
I'm just so blue

You don't know
That when I go
I'll probably won't return
Soon – you will learn.

I try to breathe you in
Wish for ultimate sin
This night
I want to make it right.

It sounds so crazy
I just want you happy
But reality can't deceive
So farewell –
        when I leave.

Polar Opposites

Sun and Moon
Light and dark
Warm and cold
Cat and mouse
Summer and winter
Inside and outside
Up and down
Heaven and hell
You and I

- can't live together
- can't live apart
- why is life so hard?

All the Reasons

When we began this ride
We had nothing to hide
And all the reasons to quit
Just didn't seem to fit.

Then we came to see
That we were meant to be
And all the reasons to love
Seemed to come from heaven above.

You had a thousand verse of poetry
To describe your feelings to me
And all the reasons for what we are
Whether we are near or far.

The depths we began to realize
With just one look into each other eyes
And all the reasons for us to end
To your brain were sent

This love is supposed to be wrong
Together we are not to belong
And all the reasons are made clear
By every rationale we hear.

The deeper our connection became
The more you needed to refrain
Because of all the reasons we both know
"We" make your heart is scared and you need to go.

You chose to follow your sensible way
There was nothing I wanted or could say
Because all the reasons you brought in
Socially speaking this is clearly sin.

You need to do what you need to do
All your convictions – these are you
And they add to all the reasons for me
That with you I would forever want to be.

Now I support you leaving me behind
Hoping that you'll never have to find
That all the reasons that we are apart
don't matter to the heart.

Come tomorrow

I don't want you to hold on
Because it seems so wrong
To adhere to my desire
When I can't help the fire.

I hope you'll understand
And let go of my hand
You just have to see
You need to be free.

My love for you still grows
This time fate – though – blows
To us these cards
And breaks these little hearts.

Come tomorrow
We'll have to follow
All I can do
Is say –
        We're through.

The First Time

The First Time
    We went for coffee
    Made me nervous.
The First Time
    You touched my hand
    I trembled and felt strongly
The First Time
    You drove around with me
    Made me feel peaceful and protected
The First Time
    You called me pretty
    I believed you
The First Time
    You kissed me
    Took my breath away
The First Time
    You said "I love you"
    I gave you my heart.
The First Time
    You held me so tight
    You conquered my soul
The First Time
    You said "meant to be"
    I knew you were right.
The First Time
    You said we'll end
    I was stunned.
The First Time
    You can't follow through
    Will be with me and you.
I hope –
    And for the first time:
    I pray;
    For us.

With Me ...

Sometimes
>   Amazing happen to us
>   Most often
>   When we least expect it.

Often
>   Have I felt there should be
>   More to life
>   Than what I was doing and feeling.

Sometimes
>   I felt there was someone
>   Out there
>   Whom I was supposed to meet.

Often
>   Have I lost hope in love and life
>   Going on with
>   Daily chores – like a machine.

Sometimes
>   In the happiness I have found
>   I wonder
>   If I should have seen it coming.

Often
>   I go back in my mind
>   To when we met
>   And the magic was right there.

Sometimes
>   I am amazed and scared because
>   How long
>   Can this amazing connection last?

Often
>   You tell me we'll soon end
>   Because of
>   The circumstances of our lives.

Never
>   Did I anticipate this love
>   I feel

        For and from you – every day.
Always
        Is the word I use
        - often now --
        to let you know
        that I am bound to you for life.

Heaven ...

Your voice
Your laugh
Your words
Your eyes
Your look
Your hands
Your breath
Your kiss
Your touch
Your embrace ....

make me feel
      -- I'm in heaven.

Can't help myself

I can't help myself around you
There's so much I want to do
The anticipation seems to be killing me
Because so close I want to be.

The power you have over my heart
I've known it from the start
And then I touch your hand lightly
I move my fingers up your arm – slightly

Slowly and softly our lips meet
That is just so wondrously sweet
We kiss so tenderly and long
To each other we seem to belong

While locked in a kiss
Your hands touch me—like this
My hands move underneath your shirt
Yours are playing with my skirt.

Your begin to sigh – softly a bit
The fire again has been lit.
Once again we begin to slowly study
The forms of the other's body.

Your lips move to my neck now
It's amazing to me how
You know just what to do
Where to let your fingers, lips go.

At times I can only hold on
Because for this and more I long
Then I kiss your neck and chest
I think you like that best.

Instead of fulfilling our desire
To quench this lasting fire
At least one time without confines
Can't wait to cross those lines.

When I take off all your clothes
To kiss you wherever my desire goes
To bathe in the glory of our love
That was sent from somewhere above.

Conditioning

From the day
We are born
Parents tell us
Right and wrong.

From the day
We are born
Our family provides us
examples for living.

From the day
We are born
Society shows us
Values to live by.

From the day
We are born
Society leaves us
Little escape.

From the day
We are born
We are conditioned
To be controlled.

From the day
I met you
Society's order
ceased to matter.

From the day
You realize
We can escape
Our social conditioning
From that day on

We will pursue
Happiness and love
As laid out by nature.

Lonely too long

Sitting
In a donut shop
Sipping
On a good cup of tea
Eating
An outstanding donut –

Alone.

Walking
The streets of the city
Looking
At the windows of shops
Admiring
The beauty of a new place –

Alone.

Sitting in a restaurant
Watching
People go by
Wondering
What to eat and drink
Enjoying
The warm and cozy atmosphere –

Alone.

Spending
A lot of my time
Thinking
About the future
Dreaming
About what may be –

Alone.
If I am doing all this
Alone,
Then I begin to wonder:

Why am I married?

Emotions amok

Minute by minute,
Day by day,
I am

Torn
Between right and wrong
Torn
Between left and right
Torn
Between feeling and numbness
Torn
Between truth and lies
Torn
Between yes and no
Torn
Between "wants" and "shoulds"
Torn
Between coming and staying
Torn
Between all and nothing
Torn
Between myself and me
Torn
Between life and death
Torn
Between joy and sadness
Torn
Between jealousy and faith
Torn
Because you said you loved me.

Ever Since

Ever since
    You first said my name
        -    sweetly
    I didn't want
    Anyone else to say it.
Ever since
    You first touched my hand
    I didn't want
    Anyone else to touch it.
Ever since
    Your first started to discuss things
        With me
    I didn't want
    Anyone else to talk to me and share.
Ever since
    You first kissed me
        -- softly
    I didn't want
    Anyone else to kiss me.
Ever since
    Your hands first touched my body
    I didn't want
    Anyone else to touch it.
Ever since
    I first fell into your arms
    I didn't want
    To be in anyone else's arms.
Ever since
    I first felt your breath on my skin
    I didn't want
    To feel anyone else's breath.
Ever since
    You first said "I'd kill for you"
    I didn't want
    To hear it from anyone else.

Ever since
> We first sat in amazement
> at what we were feeling
> I didn't want
> To sit with anyone else.

Ever since
> You
> There's no one else
> For me

The Road

You picked me up
To take a little trip
To, I don't know where
On a long, long road.

You hope the road
Will bring us closer together
As we drive along
Mile after mile after mile.

You drive the miles
I sit there next to you.
With each passing mile
On this long, long road.

I realize my road
Is a long one leading me
To someone else
Who picked up my heart
After you broke it
On our long, long road.

How not to end?

Right from the start
I knew –
      You could break my heart
You know –
      Maybe I could do the same,
           to you.

We both realized
- immediately
when we looked in each other's eyes
- spontaneously
that this was no game.

You broke down the walls
Slowly
And we allowed each other to fall
Passionately
Into this love so unique.

The love we share is so deep
 - you're afraid
what will happen if we were to leap
- In spite of the odds
And let our love come to a peak.

I don't know what I can do
To make you see
That you want no end, too
Even when you insist
That the end is approaching fast

In spite of all there is
- We know -
What we have found is bliss.
So my love

Be fair and let us last.

We've taught each other a bit
And I know
It is simply wrong to quit
So let me show you how:
        Not to end.

Forbidden fruit

Love
- sometimes happens
unexpectedly -
in weird places
against common sense

Love
- can take you by surprise
when you least expect
are not really sure, you want it -
or deserve it

Love
- sometimes drive you crazy
just when you think you can handle it,
it will put you in your place
and spin you all around

Love
- can make you smile
and your heart sing in storms
believe in endless possibilities
longing for just one look.

Love
- sometimes is so deep
that you can feel the other
know when they'll call
feel when they're near

Love
- is a wondrous thing
to be treasures at each instance,
even if the love you feel
is a forbidden fruit.

Hard to Bear

I was sitting outside
I was enjoying the light
I was pretty, nice and warm
But inside I felt a storm.

Something was happening to you
I feared what you were going through –
I knew where you were
It all was hard for me to bear.

You had called before you went,
My love I wanted to send,
Your voice had faltered
I knew your position would be altered.

At my place I got your mail
You would have to bail
Out of the love you had shown,
Just as I had known.

Thought I disagree,
You are unable to see
That all the blame you are taking on
May not to you alone belong.

Every day you do your very best
And are always taken to the test,
Now, perfect you may not be
Except - you are to me.

We know, life isn't always fair
And sometimes seeing you try – is hard to bear

After all the good you've done
You deserve a place in the sun.

Miracle

A Miracle
Is supposed to be
    Unexplainable
    Heavenly
    Helpful
    Free
    Unexpected

A Miracle
Is aligned with
    Religion
    Saints
    Improvement
    Sacrifice
    Selflessness

A Miracle
Can also be
    Beautiful
    Soothing
    Calming
    Exciting
    Engaging

My miracle
Appeared to me
    When I least expected it;
    When I most needed it;
    Makes me happy – inside out
    Protects me all the time

My Miracle
    Is you.

When you look at me

First, I shiver,
then I look away,
then I blush
wondering -- what you see.

Second, I stop thinking
then I look up.
then I walk to you
trying to see - what you see.

Third, I'm hypnotized,
then I feel special,
then I touch you
wondering – what you see.

Fourth, I just am,
then I feel your hands,
then I taste your lips,
trying to see – what you see.

Fifth, I continue to be,
simply woman,
simply in love,
wondering – what you see.

I don't understand
What you see
When you look at me.
I don't understand
What you see - in me
When you look at me,
Talk to me,
Whisper to me,
Hold me –
All I understand

That you are special
To me.

Never Before

I saw you
        But I did not see you.
You saw me
        And you really saw me.

You took a step
        In my direction
I began to see
        And my heart began open

I began to trust
        So quickly,
        -   as never before.

We talked
        About everything
We established
        Such honesty and trust

You took a step
        In my direction
I began to see
        And my heart was captured

I began to love
        So deeply
        -   as never before

One Dance

Music
In the background
Sitting, trying to work
Only the cats around

Music
Begins to make my fingers move
Without me realizing
Moving my legs and arms

Music
Takes me away from the world
That I have created
To protect myself
With only the cats around

Music
Takes hold of my body
As I let go -- of my soul
And my whole body

Music
Has me move unexpectedly
I don't even realize but
    -- suddenly --
I'm in the middle of the room

Music
Grabs my heart and soul
For minute I escape the world
While moving
    -- instinctively, eyes closed --
to the words and melody

Music
Is a part of me, my life
That's when I realize
Our dance this summer was everything

Music
Is part of us
But one slow dance in your arms
Being woman – completely -- that would have been
        One dance to remember.

Physically and emotionally

Physically
    Side by side
    With him.
Physically
    Smiling and laughing
    With him.
Physically
    Taking this trip
    With him.
Physically
    Letting my hand be held
    By him.

Emotionally
    Side by side
    With you.
Emotionally
    Smiling and laughing
    With you.
Emotionally
    Taking this trip
    With you.
Emotionally
    Letting my heart be kept
    By you.

Spring and Summer – Breaking Point

The end of March this year
Was a wondrous time
In spite of all my fear
I let you into my world.

In April I opened my heart,
It was filled with excitement and joy,
Which was not easy at that start,
Then it blossomed into love.

In May we could easily see
That the love we had found
Was clearly meant to be
In spite of social norms.

In June, though, you began to withdraw
While our love intensified
You keep pointing to the one big flaw:
You are married.

In the middle of June you began to make clear
That from your view and belief
Our end would have to be near
As the guilt came crashing in.

In July we tried to be more apart
But the magic is still there
It's breaking my heart
Thinking about giving us up.

In the end of July, I still know
That the love I have for you
I cannot help but show
Every day and every way.

As August approaches fast
This fate and love still has us in awe
And I wonder why we can't last,
With what in each other we found.

As September looms on the horizon now
I know your reasonable plan
And to your wish I promised to bow
Though, you and I are meant to be.

Surprise Attack

I was smiling in my world,
At everyone who met me,
Wherever I went,
Everything was fine.

I was the spirit in my world,
There to lift up spirits,
All around me
Everything was fine.

I was stable in my world,
A rock to others around me,
There whenever needed
Everything was just fine.

I was content in my world,
A solid persona everywhere,
Excelling in my job
Everything was just fine.

I was respected in my world
A strong, confident woman
Standing by my man,
Everything was just fine.

I was depressed in my world.
Lost and confused,
Angry and lonely
Nothing was fine.

You approached me,
In my weary hours
In a surprise attack,
    - and showed me love.
Now, I am happy again.

Timing

At a time
When I needed something
I was not able to search for

At a time
When my life was falling apart
Without anything I could to

At a time
When my life seemed to be going well
Without anyone noticing the deficiencies

At a time
When I was ready to exist
Instead of living and feeling

At a time
When I least expected it
You came into my life
And showed me
That someone could care about me –
Deeply --
At least for a little while.

Trembling

I tremble
> In anticipation
> Of your voice.
I tremble
> With excitement
> When you call

I tremble
> In anticipation
> Of your mail.
I tremble
> With excitement
> Reading your words

I tremble
> In anticipation
> Of seeing you.
I tremble
> With excitement
> When you walk up to me.

I tremble
> In anticipation
> Of what will happen next.
I tremble
> With excitement
> When you touch me

I tremble
> Because
> You've put my heart and soul on fire
> Like no one ever has…

So … I tremble

Until Then

You have no idea
How much I fear
To have to let you go.

I am sure in your heart
Because you are quite smart
This fear you know.

You brought me light
and without a fight
you broke down my wall.

The words you softly said
Made my smile and so glad
That I knew I would fall.

We have a love so deep
That it's worth to keep
Even in the situation we're in.

With the connection we share
Giving up would be hard to bear
Yet, together like this we can only win.

You asked me before
Do I maybe would like more?
Sure, if feasible I'd like to reach the sky.

Being with you has brightened my day
And if it was easy we'd have it another way
And into our future we could quickly fly.

Until then, though my love
I can wish upon the starts above
And still be with my Marine

In the way that our lives going
While daily, my love I will be showing
As silly as it may seem.

To me, for now this is enough
It doesn't have to be so tough
Our love will continue to grow.

Until some day, somehow, somewhere
Life will turn out to be fair;
And love, then can more easily flow.

From your heart to mine
And we can let it shine
And not hide it anymore.

Will you?

You came into my life
>Unexpectedly
>And with a force
>I did not anticipate
>No I wonder, every day

Will you
>Call me and make me smile that way
>Today?

Will you
>Talk to me in that deep, comforting voice
>Today?

Will you
>Write to me in that direct, insinuating way
>Today?

Will you
>Come to me in that surprising, sweet way
>Today?

Will you
>Touch me in that tender, forceful way
>Today?

Will you
>Look at me in that amazing, loving way
>Today?

Will you
>Deny me
>In that breathtaking, anxious way
>Today?

Then,
> When I am yearning, longing, aching
> With anticipation
> What I really wonder is

Will you
> Make love to me
> Today

Or
Will you
> Leave me
> Today?

Breaking

When I was young
I saw some struggles,
I was still trusting and naïve
If disappointed, though,
    I wouldn't break.

In my early 20s
I had my share
Of challenging heartaches
Personally – professionally, but
    I wouldn't break.

In my 30s
I was living through
Love dying, love denying
Painful hurting and wasting – yet,
    I wouldn't break.

At 36
You came to me
And we are meant to be
If you really leave us behind
    I know
    I will break.

Writing

Writing –
One of the main means of communication
For the last few months
between us.

Writing –
One of the main ways for us
To share our days and feelings
in the last few months.

Writing –
At times about nothing at all
Just to feel close and be
for the last few months.

Writing –
Has been way to come up from underwater
When we couldn't see or talk with each other
in the last few months.

Writing –
In forms of poetry or simple verse
Showed us how felt for each other
in the last few months.

Writing –
My connection to your heart and soul
My way of opening up
in the last few months.

Writing –
Is what I want to do right now
Feeling like a caged tiger
with the walls closing in.

Writing --
Is what my fingers want to do
Giving voice to the pain in my heart
Since you said:
      I can't write anymore from here
So I'm hurting:
      And do not write anymore.

'Til Death...

In a church
In front of the altar
The couple vows their love
And dedicates their lives
'til death ...

In front of a justice of the peace
Two people promise
To respect and love each other
- when signing the certificate
'til death ...

In he parent's driveway
a young girl is in tears
while her boyfriend leaves –
she professes her love
'til death ...

In the courtroom
The husband looks around
As he lets go off his wife
That promised to stay
'til death ...

In the living room
You look at your spouse
And realize that sometimes
Nothing can last
'til death ...

In my world
I look in your eyes, think of you, feel you
And somehow I feel, I know
We're meant to be
'til death ...